*L*ook for a

Look for a Field to Land

p o e m s

Elaine Preston

Bridge Works Publishing Company
Bridgehampton, New York

For the original members of the Wordsmith & Co.
Writing and Performing Ensemble —
Lynn, Carol, Vinny, Steve, Joann, and Bruce —
and for Mike Miller

All rights reserved under International and Pan-American Copyright Conventions. Published in the United States by Bridge Works Publishing Co., Bridgehampton, New York. Distributed in the U.S. by National Book Network, Lanham, Maryland.

Printed in the United States of America

10 9 8 7 6 5 4 3 2 1

First Edition

Book and cover design by Edith Allard

Library of Congress Cataloging-in-Publication Data
Preston, Elaine
    Look for a field to land : poems / Elaine Preston. — 1st ed.
        p.   cm.
    ISBN 1-882593-06-5 (pbk.: alk. paper)
    I. Title.
PS3566.R3983L66   1994
811'.54 — dc20   94-7129
                                  CIP

Acknowledgments can be found on page 74.

Contents

three

*E*very Valley Thing

one

Dark, Shining Water

Sometimes April heat descends sudden
surprising my cold bones navigating
along in newyorkwinter ways not allowing
the Southern wall of heat that wiggles
& slithers as I ease down asphalt now
in that old molassesmagic way.
Burning sky pours over newgreen trees
onto brambles budding with summer lifting
me slow as cloudrhythms of birdwing to memory.

There, nearest shade trees wave over
a screened porch where I pull up a chair,
lean into it, sip long from a waiting glass
of ice water that those unpausing in bright sun
mistake for Southern Comfort. I coil up
jellyfish tight, pour myself into old stories,
dive deep down & float over pointed shells
& crabs & little biting fish on the bottom,
then holding my breath, surge for the surface,
break water all in a rush & suck in long, deep mouths
of heat before I can come back to breathing.

Heat Wave

Heat wave got a mind all to its own
dragon-breathing loveself, beginning round cactus
in puffs, taking mouthbites of prickly spines
& sweeping its coiling tail over flat sand
curling into rims. It roars a river of heat
through hills so old they forget why they come
to be standing in desert when once they boiled
live & liquid beneath crust. The burning
starts roiling out, trilling with unfamiliar winds
over mountain, intimate tongue licking
bluffs redgold & pitting rock till it holds
pockets of proud sun. Pebbles glisten like eyes
glazed from longstraining at sky for answer.
Then, heaving ribs, it lunges next at plains
& little towns faceless as cliffs flattened
by glare they cannot name. It looms rare,
like desert rain come to those daring
to walk its hot breath & lift hands to sinews
flowing with light. Touch easy the air of it,
its skin tentative as cloud, while you stretch
into tall sky as far as eyes will take you.
Climb all the scaly height of wishes, yes,
but every blade of day that's you, every shadow,
belong to those who've tasted cold & night,
who still have heart & sun & moon to fall
over, under each surprise of weather.

Along Route 41

In South Carolina along Route 41
momentary summer children
dusty with sand baths
dart in their dreams
under the one stately live oak
beside the shack.

Clad only in underwear,
sometimes standing to stare
at the New York car
they curl their toes
in rake-whorled yards
then wheel to pine-cone battles
ditch-water odysseys

with no toy
but the world.

Leonie

She rocks on the porch   bunching down into the dark   sea birds
calling   99° today   too hot for Charleston Octobers   should be
cool   cool to quiet crickets a-singing   then she could finally
bolt the door   anyway   no one's coming

ought to be cool   she snaps to no one   dragging on her cigarette
flicking ashes onto sundried grass   & crunching over lawn after
a shining speck   maybe a quarter   only mica-flash on starlit
pebbles   anyway   she never finds nothing

she rocks on the porch   tucking terry round her thighs   salt air
tingling   his nine years in the ground   too long   should be
another, another to brush her lips a-burning   then she'd run
to the tide   & dive deep down   anyway   no one's willing

ought to be, she'd tell her ears   when he was here   coming
through the kudzu   her waiting ribbon-soft for him in bed
maybemaybemaybe   then the porchboards' whisper   & the bourbon
footfalls   & the snores   anyway   no one's loving

she rocks on the porch,   hunching hard against the moon
marshes rustling   all her tattered ought-to-bes
lifting anyway   with the wind

Where the Rainbow Goes

As children, my brother and I
played dusty kings and queens,
dirt from neighborhood garage floors
sliding like silk on our skin.
Wind brought incense from the paper mill
to our salt marsh kingdom, low tide
calling us and fiddler crabs to dance
like drunken sailors celebrating land.

We begged trips to the neonblue
ice cream store on the road
to the Navy Base. One night the family
drove there, ordered. But my brother
protested his vanilla, wanted rainbow.
No going back, they said. He threw it
out the open car window, sat
grinning, coneless, toward home.

After college, he went west, escaping
small-town eyebrows lifting at men
liking art, Mozart. I fled to New York,
married/divorced, raised a child safe
from tongues of shame, a daughter
like incoming tide sweetens bulrushes.
But those years kept coming back
like morning crows just when we thought
we were finally spinning a good dream.

Two decades later after years of letters
and a California earthquake, I flew
cross-country, bore gifts, hoped we could begin

to be what we never were. He and I cruised
over the Golden Gate Bridge, the dare
of city bedrock heights stealing breath
away the first time I saw it far off,
and said so. He answered how he hated
commuting from San Francisco to Walnut Creek
but did it anyway, day after day
as his wrinkles gathered eyedeep.
He bought me fine Bay Area delicacies
and expensive cocktails, the kinds
he was weary of. He said he guessed
he'd just turned into a sour, cold man.

Back in flat, gray New York, I pass
electric eye garages while Lawnamat spray
seeps into grass and then the nearby harbor.
LIE exhaust clings to my hair on the way
to work, joined by ripe aromas of landfill.
I wheel down King Kullen aisles, wish
for acres of warmgreen marsh stretching
past Goat Island, Charleston skyline.
The image of his bonetired face
lingers before me by frozen shrimp.
I finger the ice cream cartons,
wanting my rainbow brother.

Mr. Happiness on the Pine Branch

outside my little girl window decorated
the morning & the afternoon & every drop
of Carolina sun with song. Not a pause
even daylight once till darkness oozed in leaf
by long leaf & closed that yakkity little beak
& his whole melodious repertoire.

But one weepysunshiny May I grew up
& was fixing to leave the South.
My year-old daughter was set up
on a mattress in the VW back seat,
& coming-to-be-ex-husband getting
ready to head up New York way in the front
with his bourbondrinking Carolina buddy.
My momma, who was Southerngood quick
as birdwing flashes by, my momma,
she said, why you takin that pitiful chile
away to where there's no birdsong & sun?

That bonelonely line fluttered under
my mind year by year right down on
through Long Island divorce & resulting
Daughter-Putting-Self-Together-Again.
Then she became something recognizable as
Yankeelark firstflying & making up her own story.
She hums it riding her bike in the streets
of Sin City where she schools now.

Today my daughter's eyeing a brandnew bicycle helmet,
the one I reckoned, looking at the bins full of white,
blue, & black plastic deathdefying headgear,

would total maybe $30 a pop in Paragon's Sporting Shop
on Broadway. It turned out to be more like $80
a head, this transpiring while we was practicing
flapping our wings in the unfamiliar territory
of mother-daughter learning the new language of being friends.

I plunked down the Mommabird dollers
& smiled to picture her soaring on wheels turning
fast & free down Manhattan streets. I still hear
daughter-not-daughter tunes full of light,
louder than any lyrics a Mr. Happiness
on the Pine Branch on either side
of the Mason-Dixon Line could ever belt out.

Crossing the River

Those days, we'd drift
down Bay Street skirting
Charleston Harbor, the county prison's
east wall winking windows yellow at us
as we tried to negotiate the maze
of back city roads to the bridge
long before the interstate's easy arch
to the Mr. Pleasant side.

Moonlight striped steel shadows
of girders onto tin roofs
of wood shacks crouching beneath.
When it was safe to come out by day,
these streets teemed with voices
lazy on porches filled with bodies.

One aged woman sat Saturdays
on her leaning stoop while traffic
lined the streets, searching
for the bridge. Her black skin shone
blue in the sun. Camellias curled
from bushes and spotted her porch.
Dressed in a skirt and bra,
she'd lean back in the chair,
the kind like a metal petunia,
arms crossed on massive chest,
and stare. She'd never blink
at our long, pointing fingers.
It took me twenty years to know why.

Other times, some of the boys
bragged of "niggerbaiting,"
hurled watermelons into the dark
along with names and rebel yells.
They'd escape over the sheen
of river as shackled to moon
as what they had already become.

Then, first moments in sharp relief:
two water fountains in Woolworth's,
each with a plaque near the handle —
White.   Colored.
The stir of air, brush
of rough cloth on a wheezing woman
lumbering to the back of the bus.
The voice of a gas station attendant
after I returned from the women's room
saying to a black driver,
sorry, the restrooms are broken.

Miles of postcard sun over and over.
Acres of green marshes, perfumed
by the tide and shrimp and crab.
Sky crooked with summer lightning,
forests brimming with birdtalk,
vines crawling in the night,
air so honeysweet that even now,
twenty years away, the thought

of it in a Northern winter
still sweetens me with longing.

But all that talking, talking
about Africa and coons and why
did they talk, I'd wanted to know.
No one would say, just those little tilts
of heads of the women, while the men
did their secret night work.
All that dark, shining water
I had to cross
because I could no longer stay.

two

Blind Headlights

Inside the Woods

The day I left him
and everyone like him
was like walking into a city of trees,
swimming into a flood swaying
heavy, spent, poised to fall.
This time, a sharp sliver
of leaf did more than interrupt
our pale times hissing like sleet
on glass. It shaped the light,
kept calling, "Come," without mercy
like a long-neglected ghost.
He would have gone on with me
in the same, bleached way.

We paused like forest curving
into cold with only one blaze left.
I wanted an end to wanting.
He stopped where leaves began.
What had long been done
blew dry against our legs,
against the extravagance of sun.
We'd squandered our days
like unwanted children running away
with tangled hair flowing behind.
"Robbed white, robbed white,"
fell from invisible birds
onto the wind's wake.

I turned away at last,
wandered, hungry for color,
into the clustered boughs.

Thick, green whispers flickered
past the sodden years heaped
upon the ground, past the notion
of winter. I would still be lost
except for the others
who told the way,
except for having
the idea of others,
except for the roots.
Even now they plunge
deep into the urgencies
of black and warm and waiting soil
rich with the everything of woods.

swallows

she fingering the neck precise as last goodbyes   not scraping
the Absolut   against the Worcestershire or tin of smoked oysters
not letting a clink escape   the boys will hear   mustn't   won't
after midnight   sliding it silky from shelf   sidestepping
the macaroni
                    no chattering brick tiles   mustn't

softsocking across the floor   slowmotion the refrigerator door
hushing the gasket   discovering the soda   now reaching out & up
up a glass   good, good   mustn't hear   some ice   there voiceless
in the freezer bucket
                    their bedroom door's open   mustn't

five seconds four   closing on the cubes   that's it, quiet
lowering in ice & air   easy-tipping glass   no splashing   unscrewing
cap inside the robe so no fizzing   dripping gingerale out
angling the rim   so it's silent for the vodka   the pounding's
slowing down   ice is so noisy   sailing against crystal
                mustn't

taking a swallow   a swallow   a swallow
                    melting into the dark
                                dancing alone in the living room
                    with no light on

Whispers,
a lounge in the Sheraton Hotel
in Suffolk County of metropolitan New York.
Women outnumber men there
perhaps two to one, or three to one,
and privately skim self-help books
like *Men Who Hate Women,*
Women Men Love/Women Men Leave,
Smart Women/Foolish Choices,
and *Sweet Suffering*

> arriving in linen, satin,
> silk-like polyester, leather, clingy cotton,
> sandals, open-toed pumps, spike heels,
> mini-skirts, split skirts, hip-hugging skirts,
> scoop necks, v-necks, unbuttoned necks,
> long straight hair, short curly hair, teased hair,
> gold chains, bracelets, and diamond studs

floating on shrill laughter of the 11 PM displaced
drinking Rusty Nails, Zombie Punch,
Screwdrivers, White Ladies, Bachelor's Bait,
and Bloody Marys, made

> "Strong please. Hard Day" and
> "Come here often?" "Divorced long?"
> and all the liquorlipped questions
> spilling soft from their mouths
>
> for the same old struggle

Me2

DWF, 36, SENSITIVE, STUNNING, PETITE, SEXY, LOVES BEACHES, FIREPLACES, SUNSETS. SEEKS FINANCIAL SUCCESS, 40-70.

Chet, whose letter was the first to arrive,
tells me he drinks socially and used to live in the fast lane
and lost his fortune when his wife walked out
but since then he's gotten it back, learned what's important
and the last time he went to meet a blind date
he walked into the restaurant, saw she weighed 200 pounds
so he was very blunt, "because I'm a real up-front guy,"
and told her he was pissed she'd wasted his time
and he likes women who have no more than 12 % body fat
because he does, and we can work out in his living room gym.

Lou, whose letter was the only one with a photo,
tells me he's never been married but has three dogs
and a lovely cottage by Long Island Sound
but since then he's got time to be enriched by a woman
and the last time he traveled in Canada
he discovered, as he'd thought, American culture was less decadent
so he'll voyage here, "because I'm current on all travel books,"
and he likes women who don't mind his sports cap in the house
because it's fitting, and we'll each value space.

Howie, whose letter was the only xerox I didn't toss,
tells me he once lived with a wife that put him last
and after her studies, parents, children, he got his turn
but since then he's going all out to find someone who can share
and he's into stocks tennis airplanes jogging Broadway plays
and his most recent woman, in between divorces, lasted six months,
he stated, and my ad sounded like a much more active person

so he knew I could keep up with him, "because I get good vibes,"
and told me he hopes I'm not the ambitious type
and he likes women who are adventuresome
because he is, and the two of us can complement each other.

And Pete, whose letter inched along in a small, cramped hand,
tells me that he grew up with high achiever caretakers
and after this, analysis revealed his obvious mother deprivation
and the last time he went back to his wife, he saw that
he was doing his Freudian repetition compulsion bit
so he acted on his impulses, "because I'm in a very good spot,"
and told me he wants women who aren't looking to replace Daddy
and likes women who have been previously therapized
because he is, and we won't be needy.

Dance of the Blue Funk Nurse

HE: You're so positive . . .
>
> she: i am, i am, yes i am, honey pie, i'll smile,
> i'll sing, i'll dance, did you know i chased
> pigs when i was ten? can shoot rifles, fry
> chicken, brew bean soup? know kung fu? fiddle
> with lyrics? i got rhythm, tap, tap.

HE: Do you like My hat? . . .
>
> she: i do, i do, your hat. should I dance faster? i
> like your hat & your smile & your job &
> your very first story ever about a dog frightened so
> veryvery much like you, yes witty justlikeyou,
> i got rhythm, i got rhythm, tap tap tap.

HE: This feels like falling down a Mine shaft . . .
>
> she: oh no no no, don't be scared, i'm not like
> those who've hurt you. tell me what's wrong,
> i'll understand, i'll listen & listen. i got
> eyes & ears to feel with, big ones, i got
> rhythm, i got rhythm, tap tap tap tap.

HE: I've thought about everybody but Me . . .
>
> she: you've been hurt. don't worry, babes, i'll
> listen & dance & sing for you, make bread
> sit by the phone, wait in the bed
> while you get a life oh yes you will, i got
> rhythm, i got rhythm, tap tap tap tap tap.

23

HE: I'm beginning to see things about you . . .
        she: it's ok, isn't it? should i move my feet
                faster? get two black bows for them? a little
                teeny skirt? me in a blue funk, you say? oh no
                won't do it anymore. no talking? i'll zip my
                lip, get rhythm, tap tap tap tap tap tap.

HE: Just don't ask anything of Me . . .
        she: no i won't i won't. silly me, won't ask to see
                you, cut you some slack? sure, go with the
                flow, won't ask a little bitty thing, i'll be
                cool, i got rhythm, i got rhythm, tap tap tap
                tap tap tap tap tap.

HE: You're all alike, wanting a commitment . . .
        she: oh no, i don't i won't. thanksgiving, no problem,
                i'll see friends, oops, shouldn't mention new
                year's won't ask what you want for christ-
                mas, both must want it, yesyes, i got rhythm,
                who would ask for anything more? boop!

the * man again

1.

I'm on the road
to 7-11 to buy a pack of True Blues
after the 1st date is over.
I buy them after stress
when an angry poem's coming on,
you know, like Pavlov's dogs,
as in *here he* (*) *is again*,
as in why was I charitable
enough to say I'd go out again tomorrow?

*'s got dark hair, a beard —
the familiar looks.
*'s a dr in Hicksville.
Tonite * arrived with Moët
from Eperney, France.
Says he's just separated.
*'s suddenly so fond of wanting me.

I pull into 7-11.
A young * on the curb sits swigging
a wine cooler. Tall *s with BMWs,
gold neck chains, tumorous biceps
drift like lost cormorants
into a restaurant rumored
a drug-buy place. Two cops
sit in a parking space
in a Suffolk County police car,
windshield facing out.
Don't see anything.

2.

Next day we're in his car.
* slides in a tape of piano music
written in honor of the greatest love
* ever had. The 1st meeting
was a month before the divorce.
They saw each other 4 times.
We go to a country
western spot where words unwind
across a video screen & you can
sign up to sing along.
* says that * used to be shy, swallows
the 1st Jack Daniels. But now
doesn't mind getting up
in front of strangers.
* enters
the song contest, does "my way,"
gets an off-key tape.
* says how rare to find brains,
looks, & kindness in 1 package.

* strikes up a loud conversation
with the next table after the 5th
or is it the 3rd or 4th Jack.
Notes Henry there at his elbow

hash been with Alish 32 years.
*'sh got second sight,
hash had therapy.
Only needed it for 6 months.

How long to reach the hard part,
I wonder aloud.

    3.

We leave, I offer to drive.
The white line, though,
zips by neatly to the left,
just as termites sight a wooden leg,
go for it.
I drag my right foot out the car door
almost
the way
I won't quite remember
this
next time
after a world
of *s
& blind headlights.

The Drill

"The toughest fish I ever ate was in Yugoslavia,"
he said, gulped a glass of restaurant water whole.
I reached beneath my chair, slipped a hand
into my bag inside of which lay flat and shiny
this drill I'd been needing to try out for months.
I drew it out, breathcareful, past the wooden leg
while he wiped his precise lips with the napkin
and continued with winning the state photo contest,
his mouth opening/closing like a gill, while my fingers
tightened, easing the instrument towards my lap,
up so slowly while the wall of syllables sank,
quivering e.e. cummingslike. Quietly now, I lifted
the metal up to the white secrecy of the tablecloth
lapping over my other waiting hand. When asked
about his lapel pin emblazoned with "L.I.C.S.,"
he explained, "Long Island Competitive Swimming,"
his mumbles floating like fish over expectant plates,
his smile gleaming like a *Rappus Nonprofundus*
swims in the dark unable to bear surface light.
I slid the drill with eager fingers onto my skirt,
while he picked at an imaginary jacket speck
and reeled off gourmet cooking, pistol accuracy,
renovated house, overhauled cars, ballroom dancing,
acting skills, and others too numerous to list.
Then he started wrapping his old wounds around him
like seaweed, stroked them more intimately than
he'd ever finger a lover, detailing this smorgasbord
of the past to the widening linen between us.

Now it was time to flick the switch, palm of my hand
ready against the shaft, so wonderful I loved it
and it loved me and we loved that menu of words
that would be silenced. Open wide.

E-Train Man

The man   riding the E-train   leaving
Penn Station   each Saturday   morning
as I travel to the luxury   of a non-
credit   French course   shuffles
like clockwork   through   the car
same left sneaker sole flopping   open
so his toes scrape   the gritty floor
&   right arm   ends   in a Chock
Full O' Nuts Cup   that he shakes with
pennies   rattling in it   as his
cracked brown lips   chant,   *please*
help me,   *somebody,*   *please.*

We·   carefully examine   our feet,
window advertisements   above his
head   for the New York Lottery, the
prudence of using condoms,   & E. F.
Hutton   investment   opportunities.
We   make absolutely certain   we do
not shrink   in the plastic molds
of seats,   just a tightening   in the
arms   &   fingers,   invisible,
near   as our neighbor just joining
the U.S.A.'s 8% unemployment   index
arriving as   collection notices   in
his mailbox   or   ringing telephone.

This man   begging   for our eyes
not to look right   of him   as he
passes,   close as breath.   Pungence
of him   offending our nostrils. Coat

ripped at the shoulder,   white nubs
spilling onto his back.   Hands &   him
smudged black.   Nose   running.
Chest coughing.   Wheezing. Coughing.
We   do not   know / want
to know
why.
No,
we all   gohome, gohome on the LIRR
Pay our bills,   crank up gas grills.
Lie   on the mattress, pull up sheets,
& weep   somewhere   below
dreams,   *Please*   *help.*

what you ask

hovers in me like
mosquito not going away
but buzzing down hungry to cart off
drops of me into swampmusk where I'll be lost —
circling, this unasked question, real as poem
pushing into world & no matter how
I hold back, it presses down unbirthed
insisting on day & paper & voice.

I'm talking California & Napa,
burntgold hills rolling to sea
while we lounge outside, Long Island chairwise,
dizzy beyond summer-rippled hair, wind-worried clothes
in our eyes' surprise of first-wanting.
Tangled sunshadows mirror the unspilled question
which your lips shape into, don't I fear
Richter scale groundquiver, as your ears open
and eyes peek out from behind stonecareful you
to notice me sashaying in valleys of words —
not scared, tremorquick I say,
because quakes pounce before you prepare
so you can only sway with the heaving land

& anyway I've survived, unsaid between us,
bruise of childhood, saltheavy hurricanes,
more moves than fingers, operations, N.Y. divorce
like flying curves into fog, my child to mend, death
of my lover, bare cupboards, nightwalking cold & solitary,
so why do I sweat anything, leastways longknown you
with a face shining out from pain
to pull into pools of open afternoon

little pieces of me poised at faultedge
watching for wings to touch skin, ground roar.

Know, man craving me, I updownsidewaysbackwards
need iridescent waterriding, the wet that
tingles all the way up past toeslegschest,
floods over talltalk, & oozes straight-singing
into little self balled up inside — boy/girl, man/woman —
we've got to lay our fears out into the sun, plunge
down beyond tides & walls & heartquakes after:
then stone by unstone, drop by undrop
we fly.

tidal wave

I'd child-dream of swimming
golden oceans arm over arm
for the warm sand of a world
I'd wake to in a shock of knowing
as blue suddenly billowing back and back
with me up in it — taller than the tallest stars
on the rim saying get out get out:

which I did tonight
curving grownup out of town
passing knot after knot of tiny trick-or-treaters
weaving onto the road and cats or rats flying across
in a bliss of ignorance for the death of my headlights
swerving to the left to avoid them and a car
leaping the crest of the hill of these days

drawing the girl to my office telling tears
of foster homes and abortion, my colleague wanting
his children but not his wife, my friend calling to invite me
to a memorial for her husband in the ground these months

of my eyes saying
are you all right when I am drowning
on the road back
plunging down the hills
of weekly offices
to the hounds of hell
which when I return
crouch wetly by the clock

Killer Turnips

After the conference in Florence
I went down to the coast.
To try again.
I met my mother's friend.
She told me on the phone
this spring he was a millionaire.
In the old days she used to warn
my brother & me what people thought
& that we were a poor family.
Belts & paddles reminded us
if we forgot our place.
When I took my suitcase in,
a big grinning picture of the friend
sat on the living room table.

There has never been a picture
of my father anywhere out
in the open, not even after he died.
My favorite uncle from Florida
had come to the funeral.
He held my hand all the way
to the cemetery. No one else
in the family touched that way.
His hair had whitened so much
he looked just like my father.
Except my uncle smiled a lot.
That was when it really hit.

The friend brought snapshots
of his garden harvests.
God gave him all that bounty,

he said, because he donated it
to neighbors, widows, & orphans.
His twenty-one pound turnip
made the local paper.
He had a xerox.
Then while we sat around the table,
he said God moved him to speak.
He started with a church member
who used to drink. But he witnessed
to this man & he was saved. He
added he & my mother weren't after
the flesh but studied the Bible.
Then the sermon moved in for me.
I was polite because he was 86.

Next day he called to invite us
to dinner, when we were
to visit my godmother.
I declined. Go right ahead, my mother said,
be your old stubborn self,
you've ruined my weekend.

When I was three, I had to sit
for hours before plates of turnips.
I'll eat anything else, I'd say.
Turnips made me throw up.

It was no use.

I flew back to wicked New York
a day early. My daughter lives
& works in Greenwich Village.
We eat together there often,
laugh, & order things like sushi,
tacos, & cactus, whatever we want.
Then ask for doggie bags.
This Sunday during lunch we talk
about going to San Francisco to see
my brother, her uncle. Afterwards,
We watch the Gay Pride Parade
& walk away from the wet back streets,
our faces rich with smiling.

cliffs: in memoriam

*(for a woman nineteen years after
the ceremony, nine years divorced*

away from the cliffs of him and her
under the sheets of night
without toes touching
her cold body, his too soon
shaking with a mythology of women
which she took as hers for
the old shadows of his heart
beating into
publications promotions
peers who hated him he said
and said and said she was too sensitive

and there they were again and she running

dry heaves
choking these lines
and the pregnancy
she wanted to hold in her hands
which he would not dream over cribs, tiny shoes
while she plunged into leukemia, they thought,
falling into knowing
something terrible between them
would never be connected
even with this child

and there they were again and she running

which he would not shower with bouquets
for the cradle of the woman to be

38

woman not passed on
from his mothers
to her from her mothers
to his daughter
she changed the diapers of
crawled on the floors of dustballs with
talked grocery lists to
read cats and food and fables and Cinderella to
laughed the color of pine through windshields to

and there they were again and she running

away from the cliffs of those memories
she fled for her life
those years ago,
the blackness yawning open
for her one foot over them already
while she descended into
the city to classes
she cried before on the train
for those months
of having to flee her too
or leap

and there they were again and she running

away from this poem
spilling onto these pages)

— said that woman running.

t h r e e

*E*very Valley Thing

This Poem Will Self-Destruct (Maybe)

1.

I would never write a poem about New York.

2.

I grew up where they spoke in smiling parables
while hiding rifles behind their backs
or in all that green reinvented daily.
Where snakes uncoiled & kudzu rustled
over field shacks dreaming in the dark.
Where ritual was encoded into our bones
& we hated New Yorkers & a good many others
as only the rednecked powerless
can hate freewheelers.

3.

One day I woke up, I was in Penn Station in New York City, I
couldn't move fast enough, all those heels walking up my legs.

4.

But enough of that.
You know about Knew York.

Something keeps me trying
to type Knew York in this poem
which will self-destruct, self-instruct,
it does not compute.
Listen: a faint ticking has begun
& small metallic gears click into place.
Be ready to hurl yourself on the ground.

My Long Island jujitsu instructor made me
practice mirror-screaming to undo
the learned-face arrangement.
I discovered "schmuck" didn't mean just "jerk."
I got to shrugging right
& pronouncing, Humphrey Bogartlike,
impossible last names, though everybody
was Vinny or Marie, so I scraped by.

This poem is trying to escape,
like a bloated marriage on Canal Street
during rush hour.
Watch yourself: glass may explode
into crystal shards over your prone body
& each finger clasped behind your head.

5.

Yeah, it might happen like you unlock
the two deadbolts & unlatch the chain, open
the door to the process server with divorce papers.

6.

In a bar of the Hunting Valley Lodge
with a Southern friend and a Philadelphia hunter
practically & undesirably attached to us
at the hip, I demonstrated the hammer fist,
carefully & regretfully stopping
it a fraction of an inch from the skin of his temple.
In an unexpected Greenwich Village subway
token line when two fluff chicks,
the ones with black lycra skirts up

to the tops of their thighs, tried
to sidle in front of me, I turned full-face,
banished them with "I don't think so."

Look: these images might be inlay
freed in the instant of the explosion.
You don't know: my name could be Odysseus
& you are here on the Hudson River with me
searching for that archetypal fish.
This poem may all be New York defense
to ward off the Poets Swat Team.

The first time I flew to California,
I went to a laid-back party with my brother.
A hush bloomed as the sister from Sodom & Gomorrah
arrived or however you remember spelling it
before the ceiling rains letters & paragraphs ignite.
I took out a match — music of gasps — struck it
my black Knew York boots — the pointy-toed kind
good for confrontations. Then I sashayed over
to that part of the room with the inevitable
six-foot potted plant & demonstrated how
to split the grand piano in half
with the side of my palm.

        7.

Nah, that part is a lie. About the match.
I liked telling it.
I like my tongue & all my body parts.

This will not be a poem about Knew York
or about liking being a Knew Yorker.
Then it would be too small even to hide
in the stamp dispenser & will probably
return in next month's mail anyway.

But this poem is starting
to simmer like a lover who writes
all my syllables without Wite-Out,
whose fingers memorize the place on the sole of my foot.

This poem is about every Fifth Avenue
& Washington Square & Gay Pride Parade
& all the improv circus people stilting by
in sequins & $100 Statue of Liberty sunglasses.
It is about a Utopia Café
& freefalling
just when you thought this poem was over.
It has found out you & I were the ones
who left that unattended black briefcase
with the watch hands inside wiggling toward 12.

This poem loves saying,
'Ey, Vinny, cut that red wire.
Yeah, the one on the right.
Guys down there on the floor,
youse can get up.
I made a mid-course correction.
Everythings's all right now.
all right
all right
all right

Ordinary

I'm ordinary now —
brush my teeth
sweat
wonder about fire sirens
worry about bills
& cellulite
& am one among 6500
county employees jarred
by pre-election talk
of a 10% pay cut —

but sometimes
birdsong lifts easy
off the pause of leaves
rolls old images
against my heart
& the girl I once was
floats out the window
tucks herself onto wings
drifts down
into an old pine forest
where she ran & sang
before tract houses
stole the trees.

When she's lucky
she can be recalled
by the poetry of air
& get back into all this
alive.

My Tongue

I like my tongue.

Its long red whips out dramatic monologues, oxymorons,
and even iambic hexameters but doesn't score A's
in tact, since often entangled with my foot. It's labeled
by students as the fastest-talking appendage in the West.

My tongue licks strawberry ice cream
into ridges and tunnels and peaks.
It lalas with Mozart in my Honda Civic
and calls "Miss Baby" to my good, gray cat.

It pokes itself straight out
in spring rains, salt air, and first snows,
hoping that the acid rain theory doesn't apply
to these moments of being a tongue.

It wraps itself around those guttural French R's
and nasal vowels, emitting streams of such sensuosity
that available male tongues in the neighborhood
snap to attention and zip right over to say hello.

This tongue, it cozies up in cheek, whispers come hithers
to break through walls, leap tall buildings — but if
provoked, clicks into the Automatic Southern Pilot mode
that can flatten New York rooftops behind a smile.

Though it drawls out stories about Carolina marsh land,
it lies still when syllables from molten rivers inside
burn its surface until the heart informs them to roll out
into the moment of words to connect what almost was lost.

That's some tongue.
I like it.

for all the granite people

hey, I was sitting here
minding my own business
starting a practice writing
to music someone like brought
to this workshop of mine
with the four of you
when click, click, click, click
boing, boing in sidles some
dude smack into my mind
like SomeBody beside me no less,
US writing our forearms off as
click click, click click
zips out from Steven's pen.
boing boing, boing boing
gyrates the mind dude in black.
boing goes Bruce's brain
between his fingers pressed
on either side of his head.
click click, click click
hey, is anybody like out there?
boing go the dude's hips
like into the wicker chair
click click, singing it, baby, yes,
& here we go, & one & two
& on into today's story I tell
of people in my class who sat
like stones while SomeBody
& I read the hearts
out of our poetry, trying
to boing boing, click click.

Knock knock, we knock on what
we'll do to those who won't boing boing
& decide we'll click click
as silent black-hooded figures
& burst open the doors
of the classroom behind which
sit the granite people, boring
their bodies into granite cliffs,
like sing it, laugh Carol & Bruce.

But I knock knock,
is SomeBody really here
behind the silence of noise
& moving lips? I weave syllables
singing it, baby & honey,
can you yes, uhunh,
or we'll all fall down,
down with every rock in the wall.
Anybody inside, knock knock?
& in the Utopia Café when it's asked,
is SomeBody in here?
& please help, please, SomeBody?
& will you come & sit down &
talk to me of SomeBody & poetry?
SomeBody's in here click click
scribble scribble yes yes
bombing that fucking wall
down to nothng but rubble —

knock knock, click click, uh uhunh.

L. I. E. rubber

twin-barrelled summer tries the locks
of darkening car windows —
unnoticed katydids abduct leaves
murmuring in black velvet heat —
summer sinks unheard to asphalt —

only a siren from the last mile
of backed-up chrome quickens
the rubber people in the late glare —
the ambulance bounces along
a grassy shoulder while adrenalin surges
at the prospect of smashed hoods —
blood thrums with thanksgiving
for the bodies of strangers —
tow trucks muscle by, wrestle
the twisted carcasses off the expressway —

the rubber people inch toward
evening clouds fat as overripe tomatoes —
their necks stretch like rope —
their eyeballs widen like rolodexes
at the spot where they are reminded
of night opening hungry at the exit —

The Weave

I'm sitting in the dining room, opening
the *Times*, seeing the article about Sewapuri*
in northen India, from which three boys
have escaped on foot. In the dark. Few do.

> *... Yesterday, I did lunch with a friend at Pancho Villa's,*
> *a local Mexican watering hole. He's recently been free*
> *lancing in New York, taking the LIRR daily ...*

These boys were sold for $50 to a rug maker
for a year. The industry thrives.
The money exceeds the parents' yearly income.
They're told the boys will be fed/sheltered

> *... We ordered Super Nachos, fried*
> *ice cream, him insisting on paying with a $50 bill ...*

Rumors of child labor are grossly overstated,
say the fat weavers. Boys, the reporter goes on,
can continue to support the parents if they
stay thin enough to huddle in the dirt pit
at the base of the loom, in their chains.

> *... He talked of a new tennis racket, me, an oak table*
> *from Ikea, the bruise-blue furniture warehouse in*
> *Hicksville, & also a rug (dirty label cut off) ...*

The children must make the knots
       very small with their bony fingers.
              — I'm trying not to look over
                     the edge of the story
                            at the floor —

... with a

very tight

weave ...

Or they will be beaten with leather whips.

. . . we're all

a very tight

weave . . .

I don't know what to do,

I don't know *what to do*

*Edward A. Gargan, "Bound to Looms by Poverty and Fear," the *New York Times*, July 9, 1992, A8.

thinking of when the bomb explodes
on flight 405 to Chicago & Austin

Cut to the heart, you say?

Okay, Doc, when I get in
my Honda, cruise the turnpike,
it arches like runway.
I rev the engine, push
in that throttle, & we're off,
me & those Walter Mittys wanting
planes racing down the last
impediment before cloud, pushed back
against the seat & then the body
tilts & what was hard becomes
soft air as we dive up & up
into 360-degree possibilities.

Before, on other flights, I feared
bombs exploding. Feared fragments
of flesh & metal raining to ground.
Feared the last blinding flash
that would reveal the bearded villain
standing over me like every postponement.

All right, back to last week.
I'm on this plane to my friend
in Texas. He's dying. Below,
a river of cloud empties
into a tidal wave of white
colored like his regrets.
End of the week, leaving
through the airline gate,

I turn for a last look.
He isn't there.

Listen, you, I've got to hang
over the earth, watch old worlds blur by
Roll up, roll out to the edge, lift off.
See, the thing is,
always, I am the one with the bomb.

lost children

after our session
while my daughter was with you
and I in the waiting room
speakers poured lonely worlds
from a disappointed singer

        cloudy days
        dreams gone by
        sad and shady
        if living is without you

once my father chiseled my first attempt
at brownies out of the pan
said *delicious* while he choked them down
one afternoon he climbed nearly to the top
of the world's tallest tree
and unwedged his shaking tomboy daughter
years later at my grown-up house when
I suggested a New York ballet his eyes
lit up, then darkened when he heard *no*

from my mother who only laughed
when the Saturday couple came for Canasta
and who trembled with embarrassment Sundays
if we were late for services or if she dared
cause trouble in department stores
but things would run tight in her house
by God the fear of whom she said was put
into her by *her* mother who spoke and you jumped
the way my father and brother and I were supposed to

but this night a lifetime later I cried
for my parents who now are old and dry,
want to go to them, say *I'll be all right.*
say *go to the city of light, go anywhere,*
say *come into my arms, poor lost children*
but I see they have always been afraid
of too much
sun

A Gathering of Flames

Teasing the tip of memory
a wind lingers at the windows
to work on the glass
shimmering in the dark of this room
now rich with smells of fresh-made soup
and fire flickering on skylights.

But I keep the silver-spun dusk
and open the door to breathe it,
walk in it to the beach down the hill
where I take up in my arms
a recent storm's gift of driftwood,
a gathering of flames from the sand there

where I cannot yet spell the meaning
of this new and strange country of now
except for these:
blue of moon-hung bay,
trembling with dried marsh flowers
still vivid on December stalks,
bare urgency of winter branches
only recently hidden by the pause of leaves,
their buds fattening even now
with promises of springs to touch.

something about red flowers & a camel

Like warm water seeping into cold —
finding myself beached in museum sections,
their French paintings — rainbow Arabic melodies
on the car radio on the way to the city —
familiarity in bronzed faces of strangers —
all this begins in a 7-year-ago
deep winter which has me looking at
Times foreign rentals for the 1st time —
the ad for an "apt i/e heart of Paris," &
it is already fact: I'll live there.

Five months later, night-flying from New York
into the next day of Paris, I'm expecting to recall
some childhood language. But after Orly, along
the Périphérique, when I try catching the French
drifting from the driver, the syllables hang dream-real
in the interior just beyond understanding. I have to relearn
simplest words — *cheese & grapes, please & thank you
& I'm lost, can you help me.* Yet, the guttural R's, hand
& eyebrow work come easy. I am back

among tin rooftops, clay chimneys rolling
in tin-gray waves of roofs down from my 5th floor window
to the Champs Elysées & Eiffel Tower.
I live in Montmartre, whose immigrants
hail from Algeria, Senegal, the Middle East.
Coppery *shiras* floating from tea shops
bring me back awake & alive to the smell
of fresh-baked bread, to glassy melodies
from three-hour feasts with olive-skinned,
raven-haired friends. Full of tears at the end,

I lift my hand to them from the backseat of the taxi,
leave what I know for what I know.

Seven years later I'm still learning French
& deserts & bought an Algerian CD Sunday.
Its rhythm cuts deep & why do I remember flowers,
small red ones the size of a dinar on the reins of camels,
their drivers tossing tunes from small brass bells
onto sandy winds blasting blue sky?
& there's a fountain & palace stones,
hand-chiseled, smoothed by perfumed feet,
clattering palm fronds, flapping canvas, a camel.
Or maybe the animal is only as real as the lives
we invent for ourselves that melt away like the edge
of dreams at first light. But there's something I know
about this camel, about slipping from the shadows
of midnight curtains billowing out onto the summons
curving from the high minaret. I'd chuck its head.
A man & I would climb up, ride easy on secret silk rustles
into desert painted with cloud. When we passed beyond
the Great White Dunes, we flew with the big wind
to the other side, my long black hair streaming,
heart whispering this day would be true tomorrow.

Collage

The day starts small, maybe as a sketch
on thick paper. Say you've drawn a flag
from the geography you're strapped into,
the cloth you can't see from far off
because of narrow regrets. Your life lies
in pieces, you're shivering in a front room,
you feel the harness tighten. Down the street
the Stars and Stripes hang limply in low light.
You remember summers as a counselor
when you were taught to fold your flag
into blue triangles, neat as vague futures
you thought unfurling technicolor, enough.

You touch the lower right of the sheet
where, inside a border the color of sand,
a pastel square whips in the white breeze:
U.S. flag, edged by a silver spring stapled on.
It spirals, sharp toward sky or dune on this collage,
or the one down the street, or maybe the one
on the TV droning in the other room. Minutes ago
you hurried to trace your hands, crayon their shapes,
cut and glue them to the corners. But now you find
you cannot rise from your chair because of them
though you smell the Weight Watchers' 200-calories
in the oven, though your tongue curls for it.
You stare at the scissored parts of you, reaching.

You try not to picture scenes stored away
from your months in France, where immigrants
from Eastern Europe turned into artists,
sketched Paris tourists at Place du Tertre,

twenty francs a head to buy baguettes,
packed themselves eight to a room by night.
Then there were days of gypsies, thin children
working crowds outside the Louvre, trailing
fat men or spike-heeled wives or ancient mothers,
waiting for a wallet careless in the sun for them
to lift while running, then splitting into three
starving lines of flight disappearing into the city.
You cannot stop seeing desert beggar women
sitting with infants on cobblestones, women
holding out their hands to you on the Champs Elysées.

You tilt your ear for the Unexploded Bomb
they said would end the Earth. You think you hear
distant whining, it is near as tattered, alley cardboard
where the underside of Cain glitters ghostlike.
Near it is, as stick men with smiles pulling flesh
to bone rigid by the sidewalk blankets filled with
ivory, brass, leather bags. It comes nearer
like sisters in the evening shadows with vacant eyes,
near as open windows where you sit despite the cold,
perhaps typing tiny words about opened fingertips.

It's hurtling toward your eyes seeing the front page
photo of a homeless figure tucked into
a rounded London window — big-eyed orphans in Rumania
staring from the Zenith — the Berlin Wall tumbling —
Russia splintering, atomic stockpiles worrying the world —
Haitians drowning, 10,000 orphaned Sudanese boys
walking away from war, the Mid-East awaiting flame —
AIDS cases sprouting hourly like weeds — pollution burning,

foods brimming with pesticide — friends whispering of layoffs —
all of this, it caves in your dreams, scratches toward day.

A shadow of yourself stares at busy hands
that would break through paper, a laying on.
In the dark you hold up spread fingers, as if
to set ablaze the night before the music stops.
Your mind fights to wake before the certainty
of sky shreds into bits of pretty-faced wet flags,
red-soaked stripes, and blistered stars. You glide out
of these words onto unimaginable air, seeing
everything, touching the untouchable, floating
into the lives of strangers, beginning yourself.

Flight Instruction

Suddenly I'm straddling a runway line,
my feet pushing Cessna 152 rudders
as the plane aims straight for grass,
comes back, blurs past the control tower.
We rise, lift an almost-ton of metal up
toward the arc of earth, the instructor
the thin link between us and land
falling below rivets on the cowling.
We sway, breathless as island shrinks,
rivers ribbon through marsh,
trees stitch fields together.
The sun hangs hazy, like memory
gliding into the cockpit —

my father's thick hands
teaching how to change plugs,
our first walk to big bank doors,
our bucking the straight-shift Ford
on dirt roads pluming brown behind us,
that first drive over the high, narrow bridge,
his lessons with hammer and nail,
but the child in me choosing convention,
our long journey away from each other:
these, touchable as the sheen of light
through the propeller blades,
these, far away as his letter
written from a Pacific warship
to me before I was born promising
some day we would know each other again —

The instructor calls for a 360° turn,
rollout. Ground tilts as we yaw
toward the landing, pitch and trim,
power down toward the base leg,
curve to the final approach.
Asphalt flies up as we roundout,
touch down, roll easy. Brake.
Next day I walk the surface,
savor the harbor tides. Clouds
trail from my hair and fingers.
I breathe in lungfuls of world,
gather up moments of air teaching me
how to float in straight and level flight,
how to pitch and add full power.
I am learning my father
and the woman he foresaw
finding the stars   again.

Hunting Valley

1.

This is *not* another poem about a man.   I've spawned
enough of those to fill a small airport hangar in northwestern
Pennsylvania.   It has to do with glide slope & ailerons
& empannage & an end number
but almost nothing to do with a man

2.

though take this hypothetical throw of the dice.   I used to.
Picture a man in a typical place   maybe the Hunting Valley Inn.
My back was to him   my feet swinging from a brown bar stool
& he was betting I'd fly without weapon   into wooded deep country
with him   & when I turned he was describing trophies of doe
in his lair   how he gutted his kills right in the grass
& hauled them back for immediate mounting.

3.

Let's say this is where the conflict always started   in that first
rustle of the underbrush.   Imagine us beginning to break
from it   run through the hunting fields   arch into the wind.
But then   his black buck eyes —   some way the moonglow
hit them   a nuance in the profile   as he was coming onto me —
something saying   this short time was the only one
there would be.   Whatever.   18 or 24 or 49 versions
of the game.   I've heard them all.   But I kept sitting
with the same figures,   plotting the same headings.

4.

Let's say he didn't know —   I didn't even know —
I'd had the Uncle Henry Schrade + LB47 knife in a leather holster
strapped to my waist for years.   Didn't know I'd been waiting
behind the leaves   feasting on all the meanings of green.
Didn't know I'd been waiting for the flash of ass, the very next ass.
Waiting to slide shining down his chest   split it   from neck
to crotch   the all too generic insides spilling out for the last
Big Red surprise.   & let's say I fed on the heart, steaming
in the open cold.   Let's say I tied the stiffening legs   brought
the carcass home   nailed it to the wall with the others to admire.

5.

But let's say those still eyes.   They had me writing midnights.
They had me naming names.   They had me
seeing my long-ago body flung off course. They had me
ripping out every one of my bloody regrets —   how I'd adored
hoarding them   how I'd fingered their splattered trail down
the long road —   let's say they had me seeing the father
of this all   the laid-out hospital father   & me direct
from the airport with my baggage.   Let's say our last
hour together   before his leap into the dark.   We saw
without saying our silences   how we had failed, how we had tried
to love each other.   His was the same steeled aching passed
down to him   as to the others I have known   our throats
trembling against the blade.   Those eyes,   they had me
gathering up every stillness.   In the bone-lonely dusk
they had me cutting loose every dream I ever had
until nothing was left   but sky

6.

until I could rise,   metal up,   from that shrinking earth
sway that hard body at minimum controllable speed   until
I could lean   silver-winged sideways   into
the unsayable night.   Though the engine might be lost
though every instrument was gone   I could lay my hands full on
come back in dead-stick   like a thing released from darkness
hunting in the valley for a field to land.   I didn't have to die
as long as I could keep going   keep falling into finding
until the last thin slit of light.

The Moment of Hawkwing

Her spirit often came, aching with stones,
to White Rock Canyon when its crest was
but a thought in flecks of mica flashing
into the distant line of waving desert.

When the world was called flat. When
beyond what her eyes could see she saw
Conestogas, horses wading streams of light.
When whine of jet, coyote, ring-tailed cat
sank to sand. She'd sit by boojum trees,
outstretch her hands, fingertips spread
to trace strata down to arroyos where rain
once called twelve-year seed to bloom.

This day, she laid a pebble warm into her hand,
its palms hard from climbing hills year
after year for that which knew her name.
Heat flowed heavy up her arms into
all the lives she ever was, into
the words of Old Ones folded into
clouds she could only fly in sleep.

Then. She who came to be Hawkwing
stood planted on the slope of rock.
Melted into planes of afternoon
as sun curved down toward the far ridge
its west slope burning red like beads
woven into black hair, like blood
braided into memory of earth.
The sky heartened, swelled with her, leaned

into a red-tailed hawk that lifted colors
high, its first small cry smelling
like salt shells left along old river,
its eye knowing every valley thing.
The hawk, the woman hung on a current.
Paused against the terror of the highest
peak of blue that oozed down upon the ground
poised to still bone and flesh and pulse.

Creased the body. Splayed the claws.
They were a thin ribbon of desire daring
secrets of deep shadow on molten feathers.
The base of the mountain rose rocksharp-near
and nearer towering saguaro cactus, prickly pear
where lizards flicked their tongues.

And now, arc of wing, glint of pinion,
up a melody of body where bird
was one with woman with the glimmer
of sand and bluff and red and rising
loop back, her mind freefalling through dreams
of hawk into flower-tender hosannas
of wind catching all her lives like wings:

It was the moment of air she was born for.
The moment when everything began to be

alive

forever.

beyond crayola®

Yankeedoodles, these surprise crayons
you arrived at our workshop earlier with,
the ones waxpressed in muskyellow
& green cardboard, they hiding a whole cast
of stand-ins just below the wrappers.
See, I wasn't done smelling them on the porch
when you first whipped them out.
I only sniffed real ladywise
like Southern women sit in ficticious
afternoons of awning-shaded homes
& wear primwhite gloves to sip
tea with honeysuckle delicacy.

When y'all left I got me that box
slipped out to the porch
lifted it high in the air, sat
down Indianstyle. Remember?
Like we all useta sit as kids imitating shadow
in pineywoods when we weren't even
a skinny thought in the minds of all-arms-
&-legs &-wind-nippled boys pumping
their bicycles down Rifle Range Road to where
frecklenose girls'd swoop out over Calabash Pond
on vines from the bogeyman tree.

Sitting I was, soft & reverent
like cat become statue
with only tail twitching mousewise
plying the full, redfeather moment.
I puffed up my chest
so all the ribs stood out

in the twilight, each curving one,
& I breathed in huge heartfuls
of honeyheavy, moonlightmelting,
crayonsmelling night. I sucked scent
till I felt mind meandering
out flesh onto dark, curling
everywhichway, sliding right down
into North Charleston, South Carolina —

home to Miz Preacher's first grade class
near the Coca-Cola plant where
when we toured it behind her lavender
cologne we got little crates
of green plastic bottles just the size
to fit in childplump palms . . .
place of the neonblue woodplanked
ice cream store where you could buy
the best rainbow cone in the world . . .
harbor to gray Navy boats
big as sky lined up rope by rope
to docks bobbing with whitesuited-
blacktied-roundcapped sailors walking
straightlegged down shimmering streets . . .
locale of the paper company
which when you're standing downwind
its sawmill pungence sneaks up
wraps round your body essence of forest . . .
site of loblolly & cypress knees
& oak arching high overhead, up to always-
summer clouds riding the Cooper River . . .

so high your childeyes filled
with technicolor dragons & whistles
& flying carpets creeping round & under
the four walls of when we were little
cruising on invisible tides of
nowbeyondnow to where today was waiting . . .

So, Yankeedoodles, those little stray
periwinkle moments, they got all stuck
to me from the longago but right-here
sepia place which I'm just this minute
back from & I'm snipping off those little
gauzyspiderwebby strings where they're clinging
fast, gentler than sugar's angelwhite breath.
I'm dropping them lilaclike into the spangle box
'neath the sill of my memory where reside . . .
pointy shells & fiddler crabs
& Spanish moss & soaring Mr. Snowy Birds
& flowing New York sidewalks & jumbo jets
at the moment of air & Paris cobblestones
& 1 cormorant on a Napa Valley lake
at Stag's Leap & molten California mountains
& hawks hanging on desert air to come
& all the crayola™ on the carousel . . . this trip.

Acknowledgments

Grateful acknowledgment is made to the journals below which have published these poems:

"Along Route 41," *Long Island Quarterly*.
"beyond crayola*," *Mississippi Valley Review*.
"The Drill," *Long Island Quarterly*.
"Flight Instruction," *Walnuts Quarterly*.
"lost children," *Journal of Poetry Therapy*.
"Me2" *New York Quarterly* (only the first half of this poem is included and was published under the title of "DWF . . .")
"The Moment of Hawkwing," *Color Wheel*.
"poetry," *Journal of Poetry Therapy*.
"the * man again" (originally published under the title of "the * poem again"), *Walnuts Quarterly*.
"This Poem Will Self-Destruct (Maybe)," *Walnuts Quarterly*.
"whispers," *Journal of Poetry Therapy*.